NAUGHTY
Coloring Book #1

M.S. L.R.

"Welcome to the dark side."

DISARMED

M. S. L. R.

From the author of The Darkest Nights series
& the Bad Romance trilogy

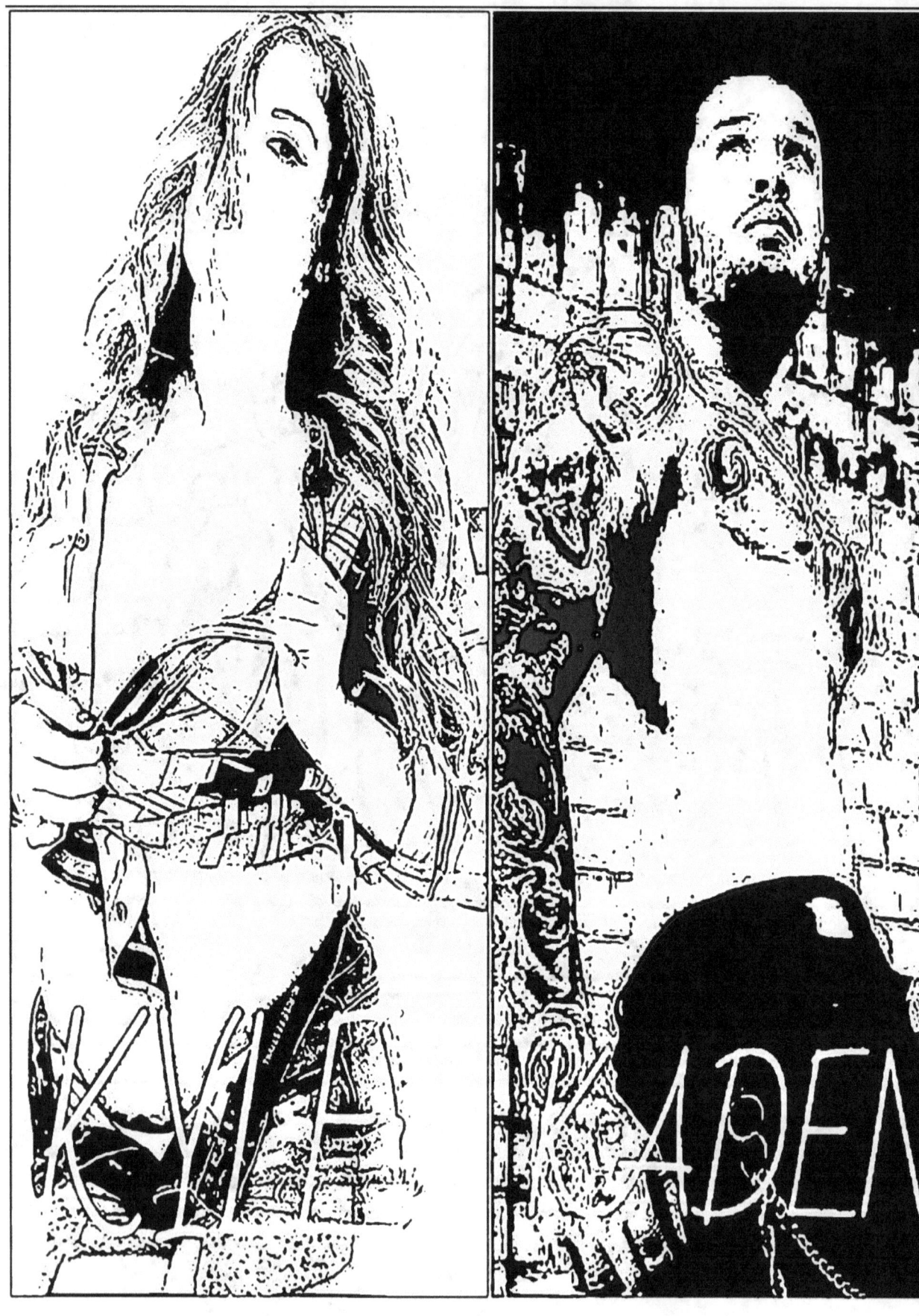

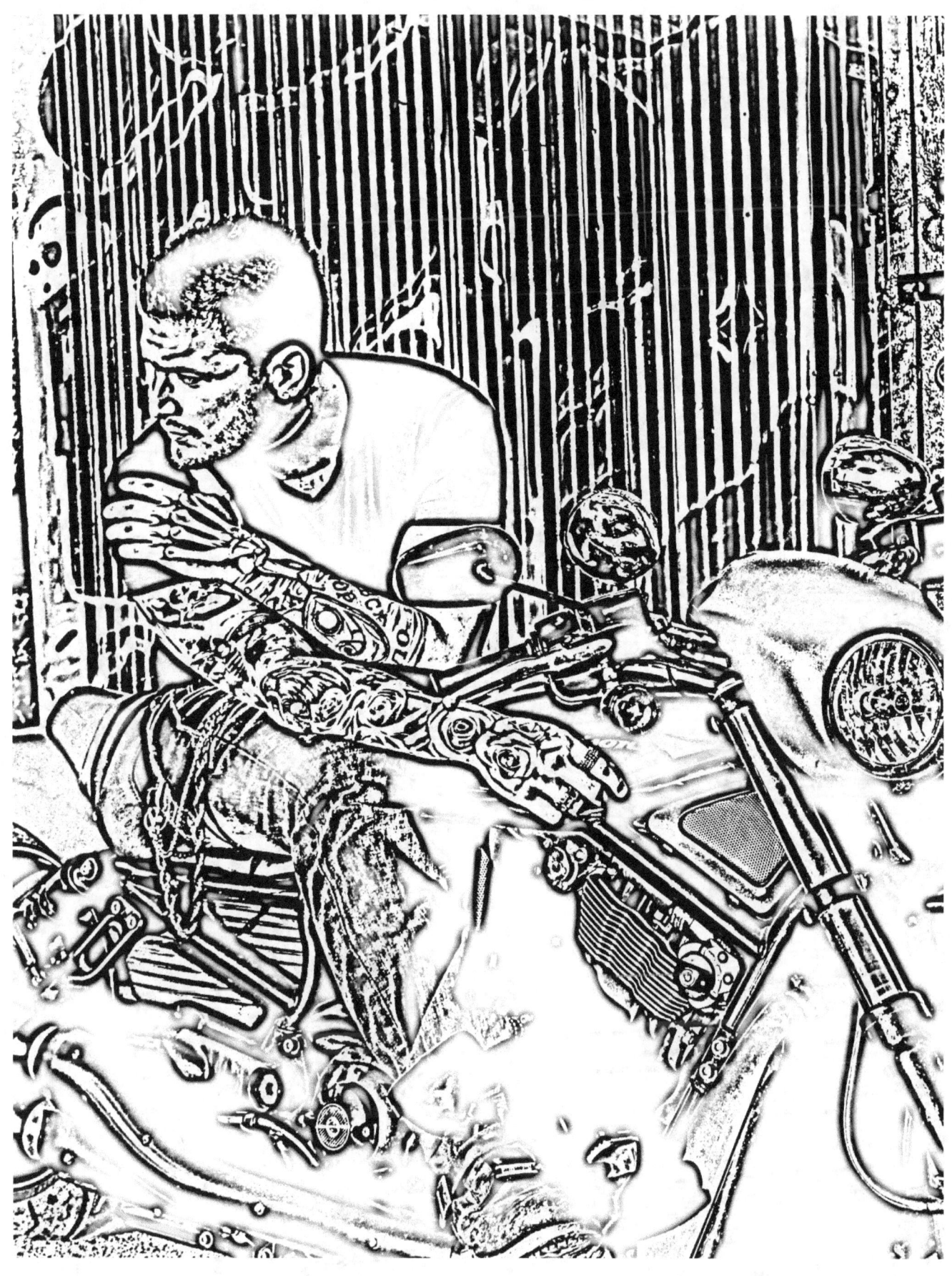

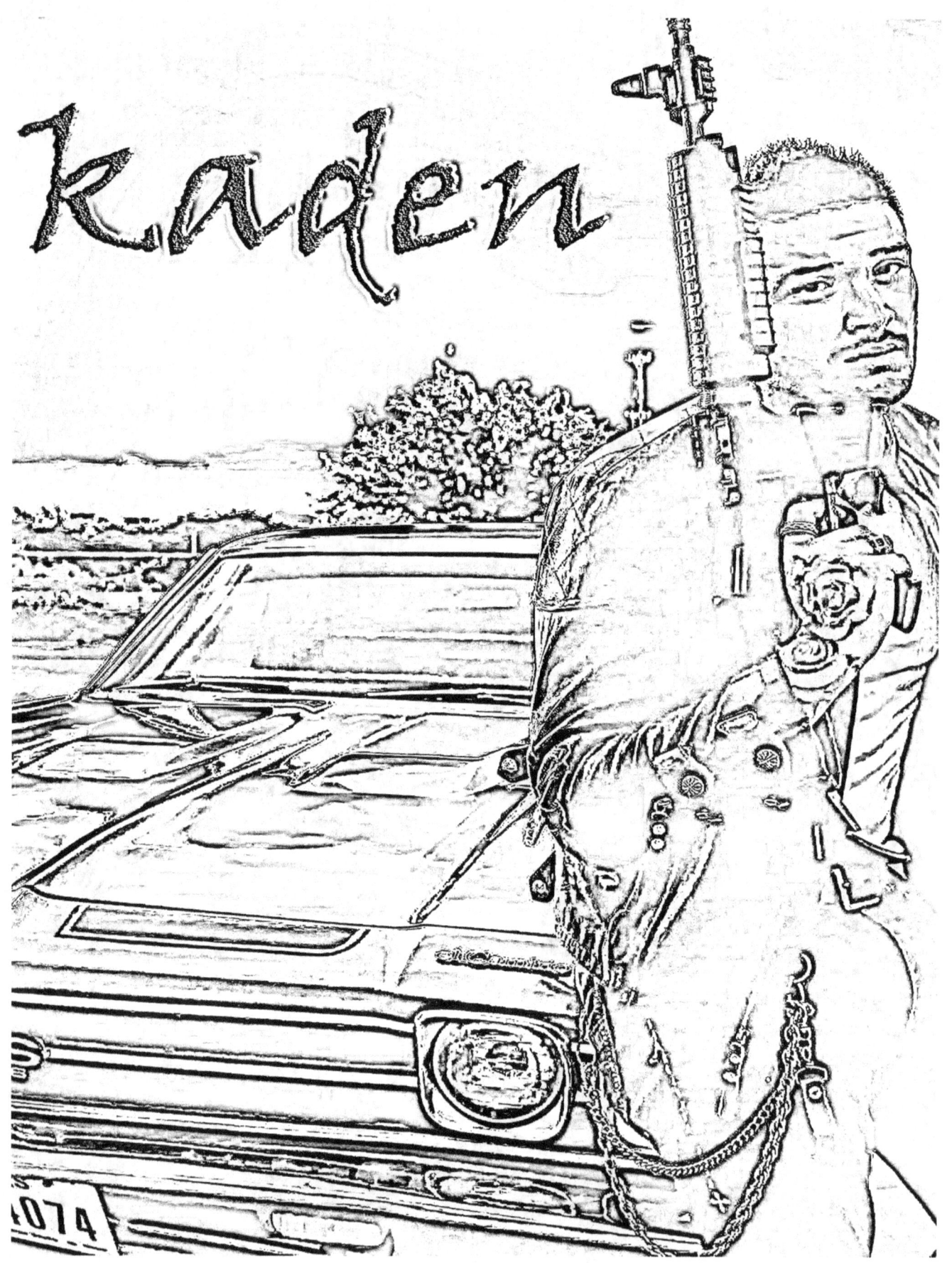

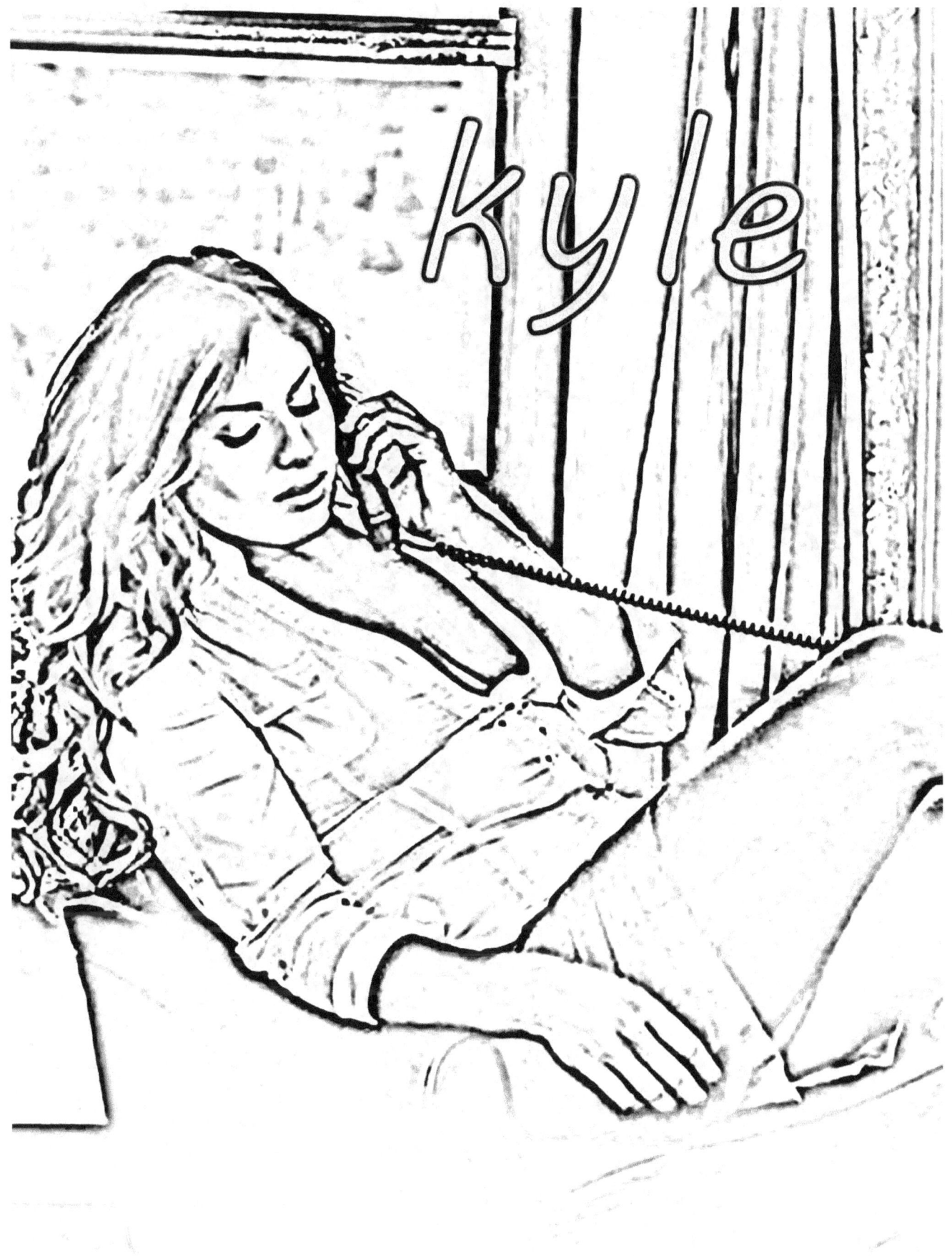

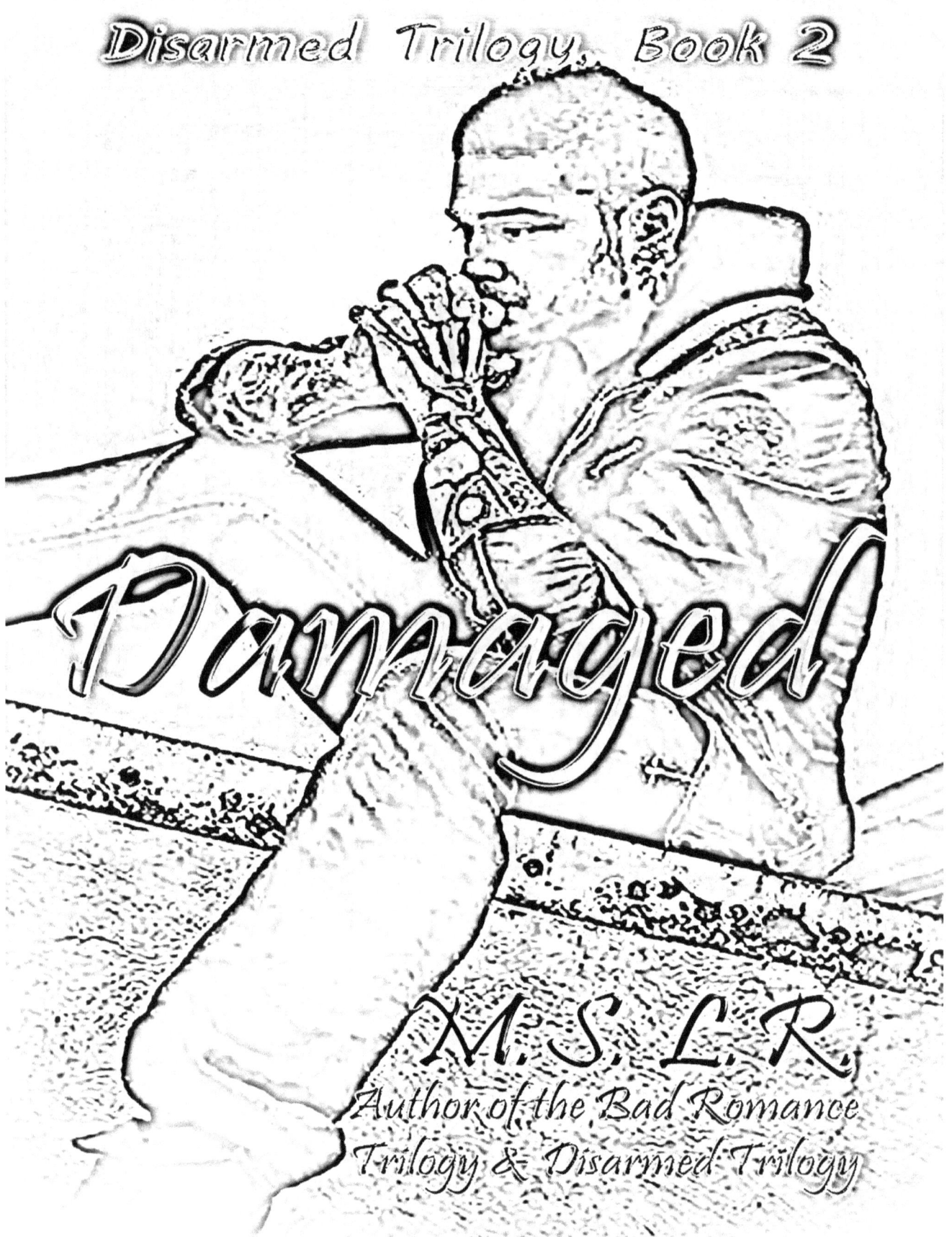

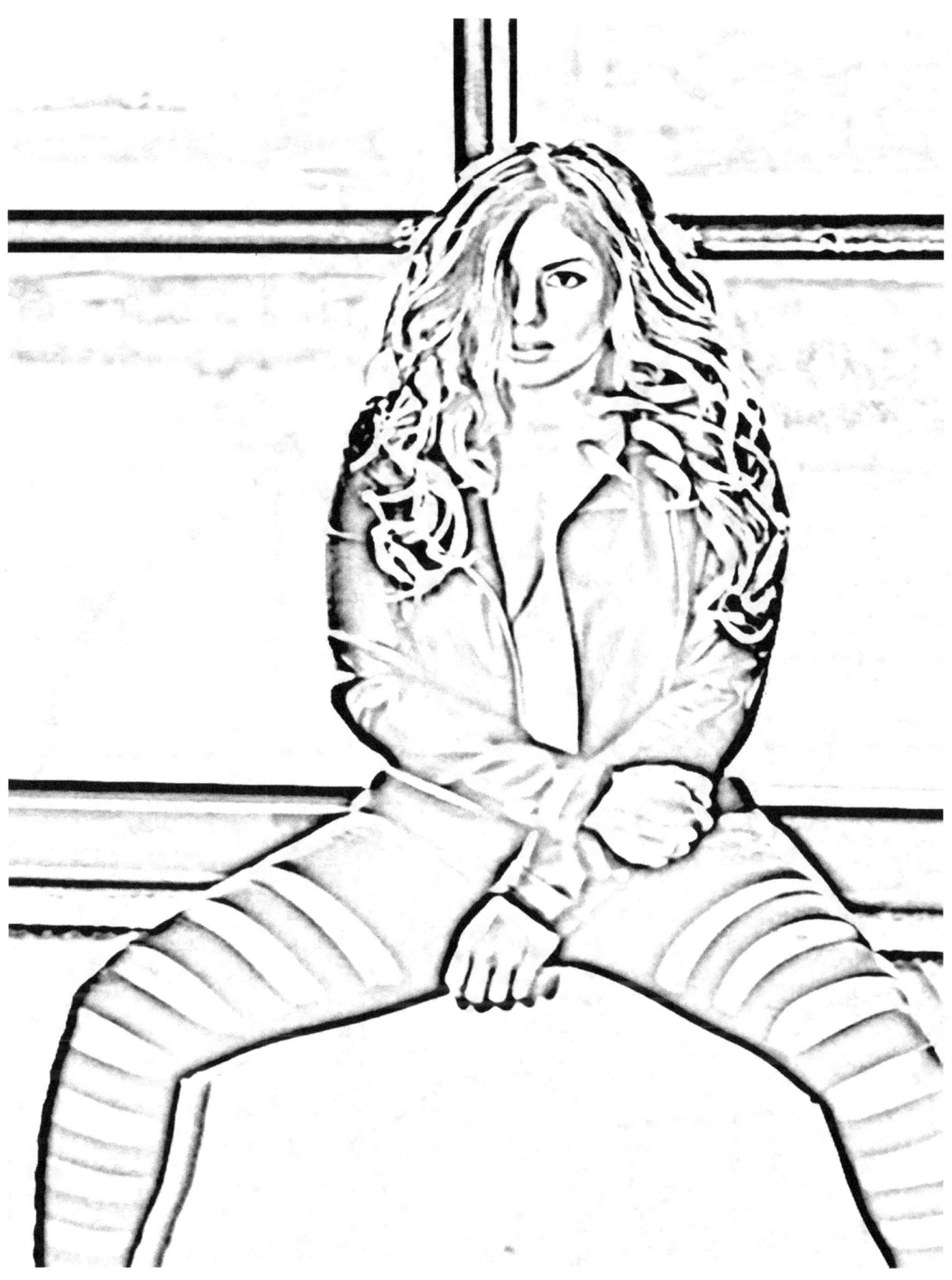

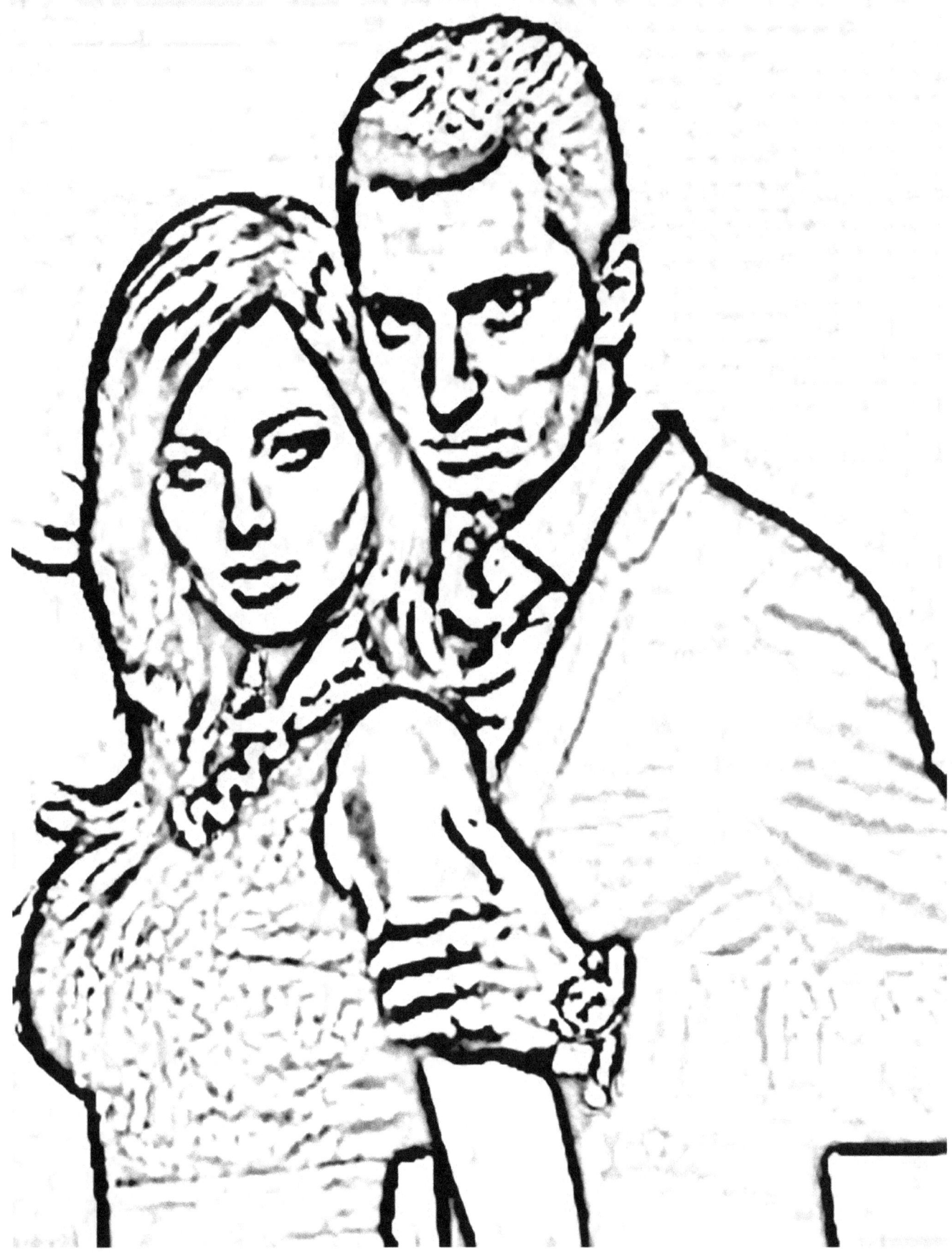

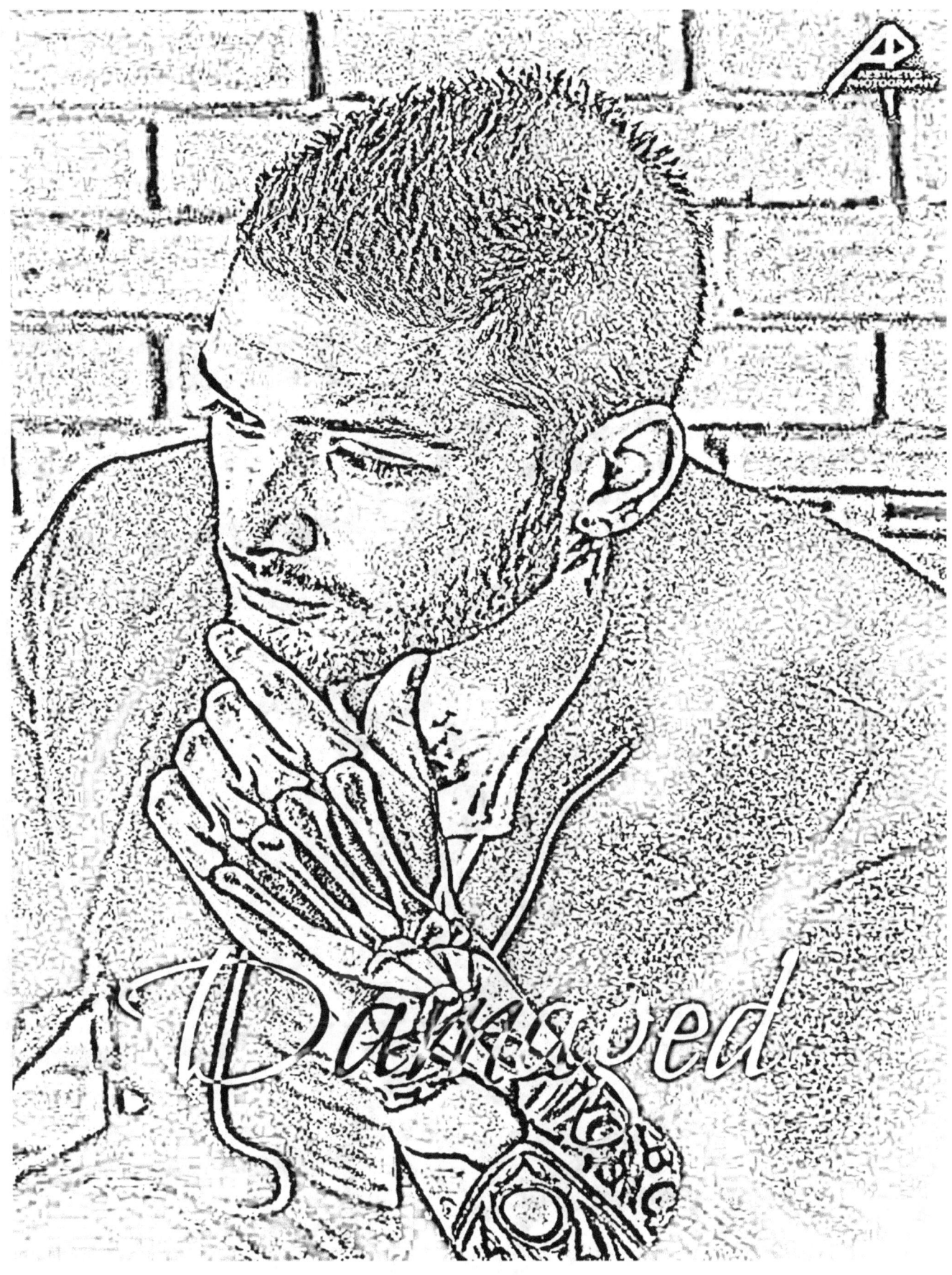

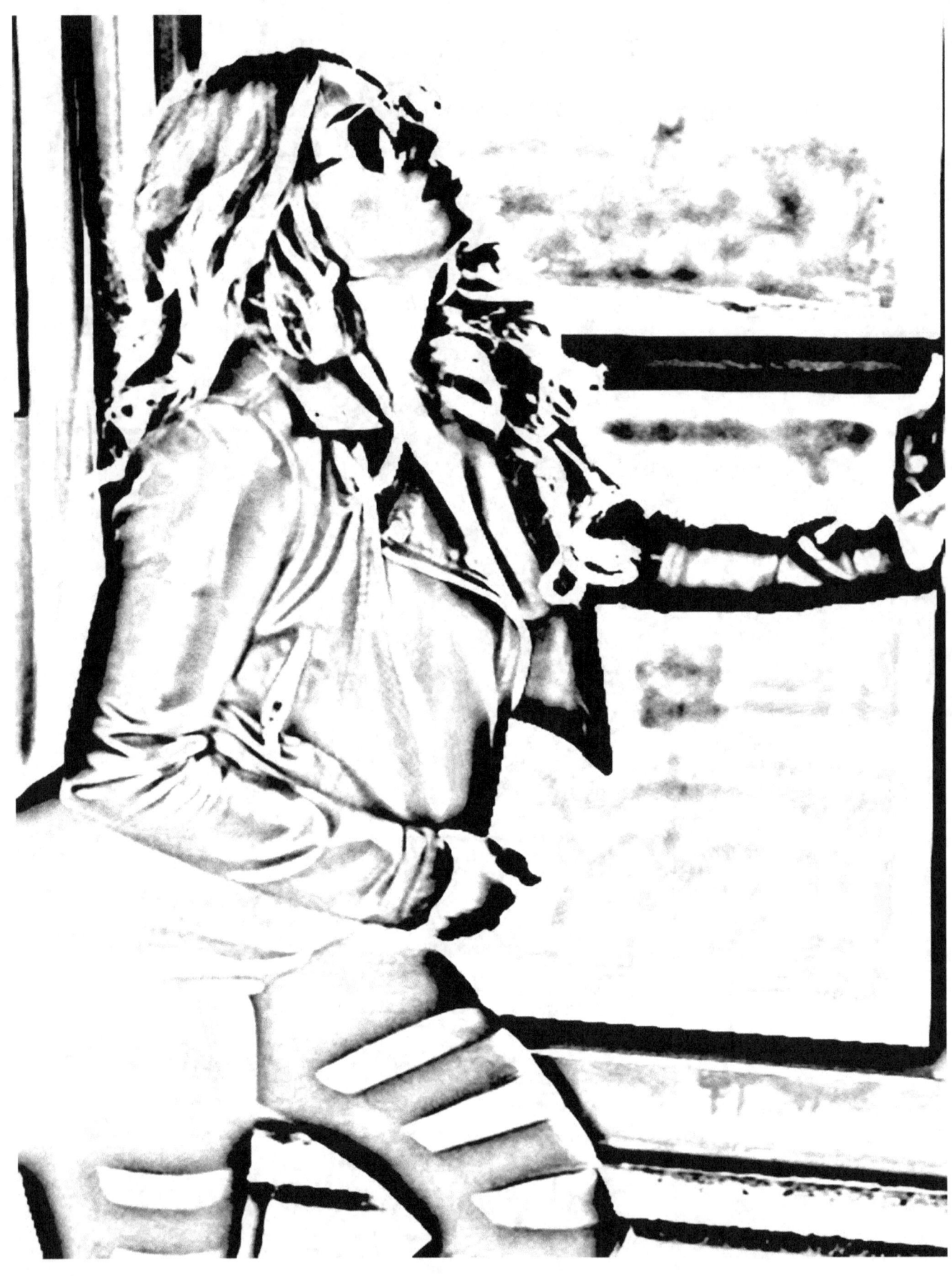

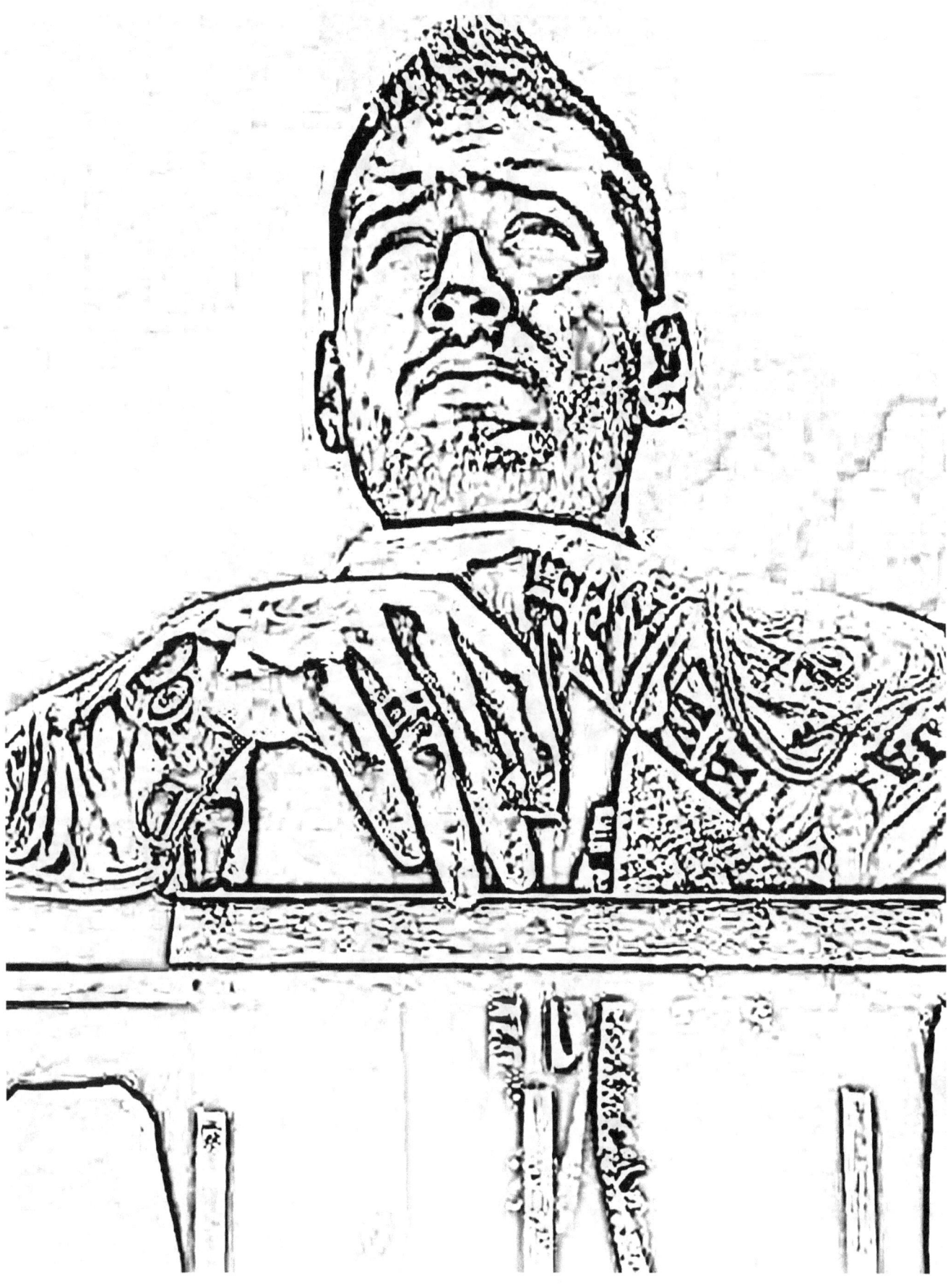

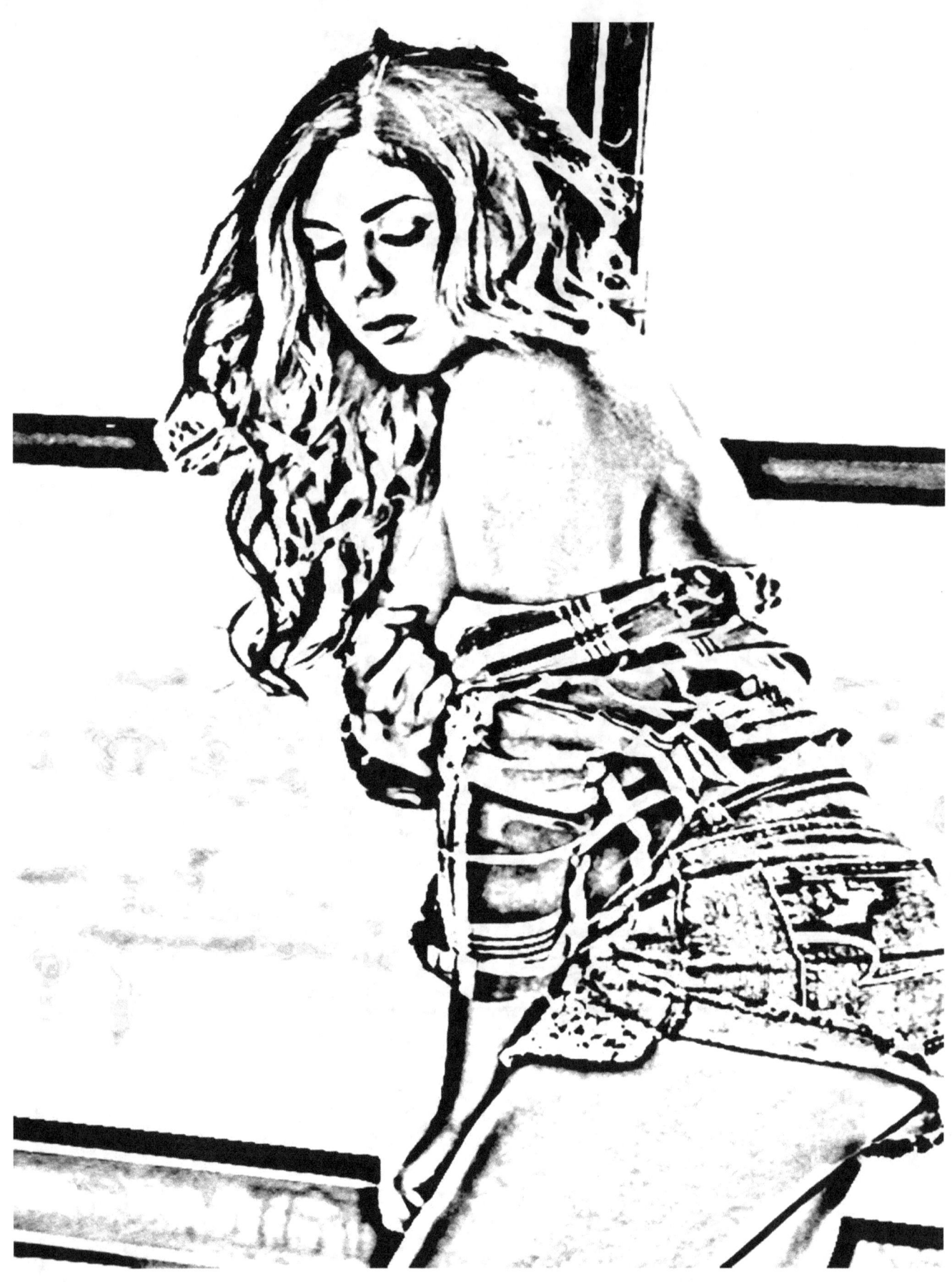

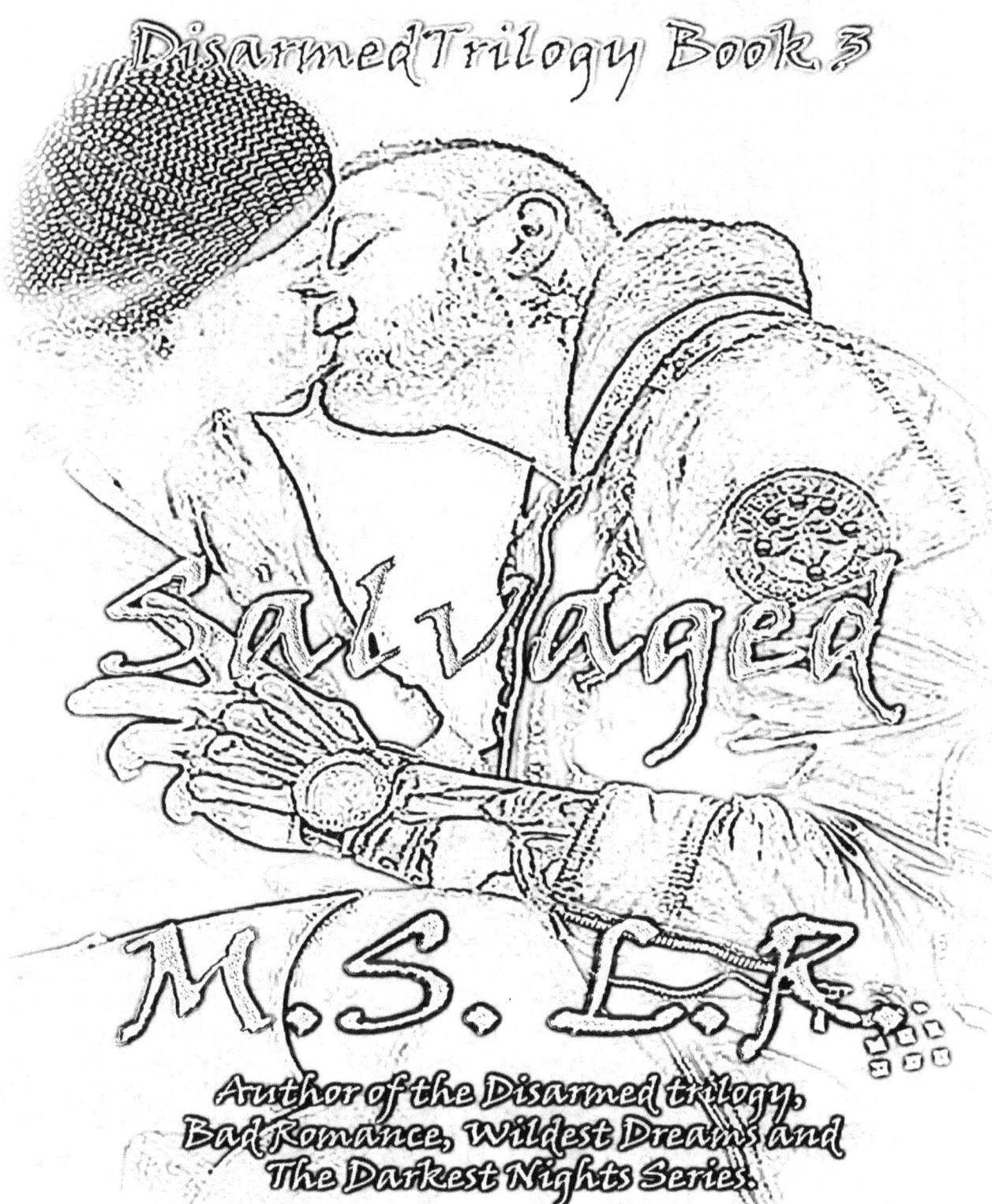

Disarmed Trilogy Book 3

Salvaged

M.S.L.R.

Author of the Disarmed trilogy,
Bad Romance, Wildest Dreams and
The Darkest Nights Series.

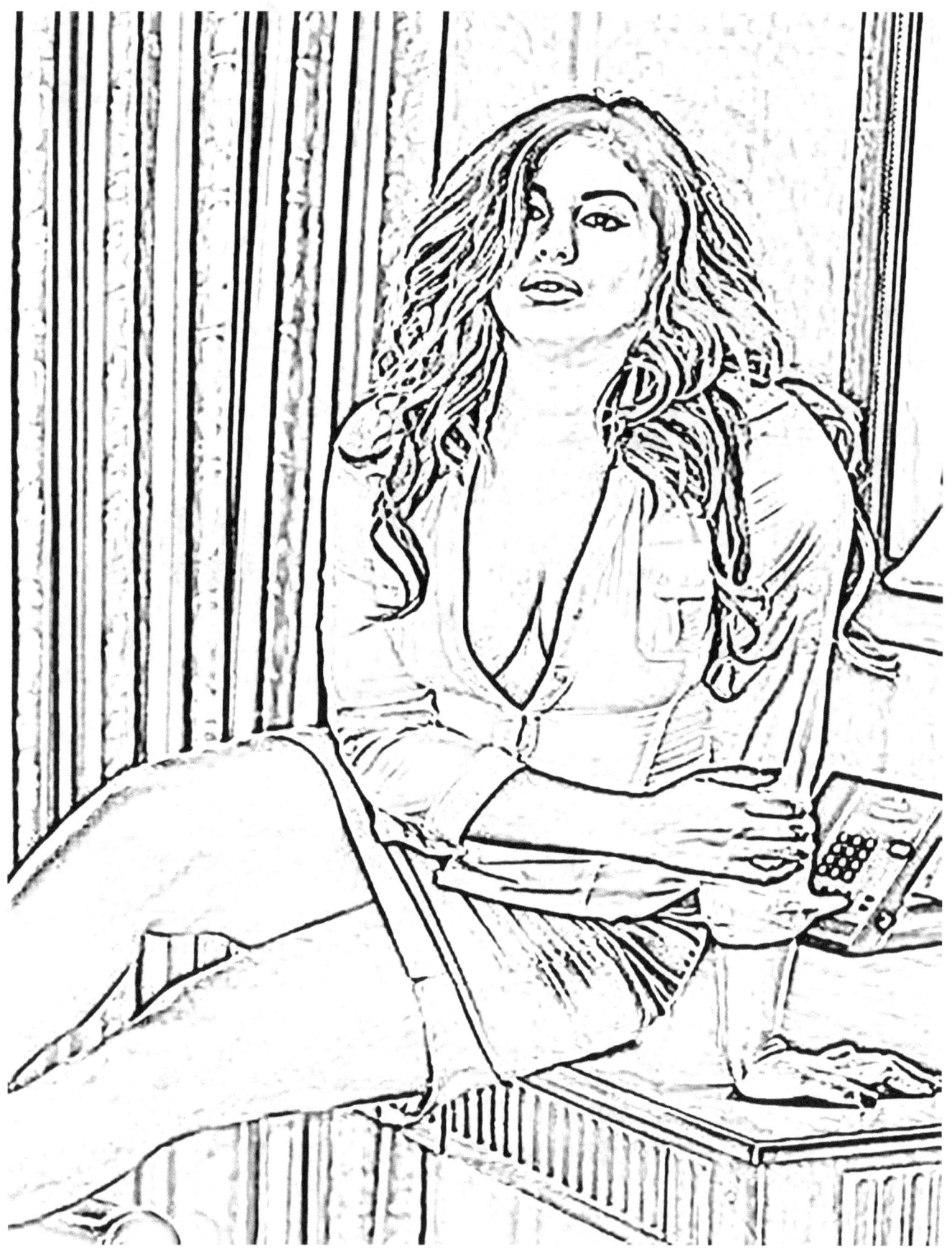

A Disarmed trilogy novella

Saved

M.S.L.R.

Author of the Disarmed trilogy, The Darkest Nights Series,
Bad Romance & Wildest Dreams

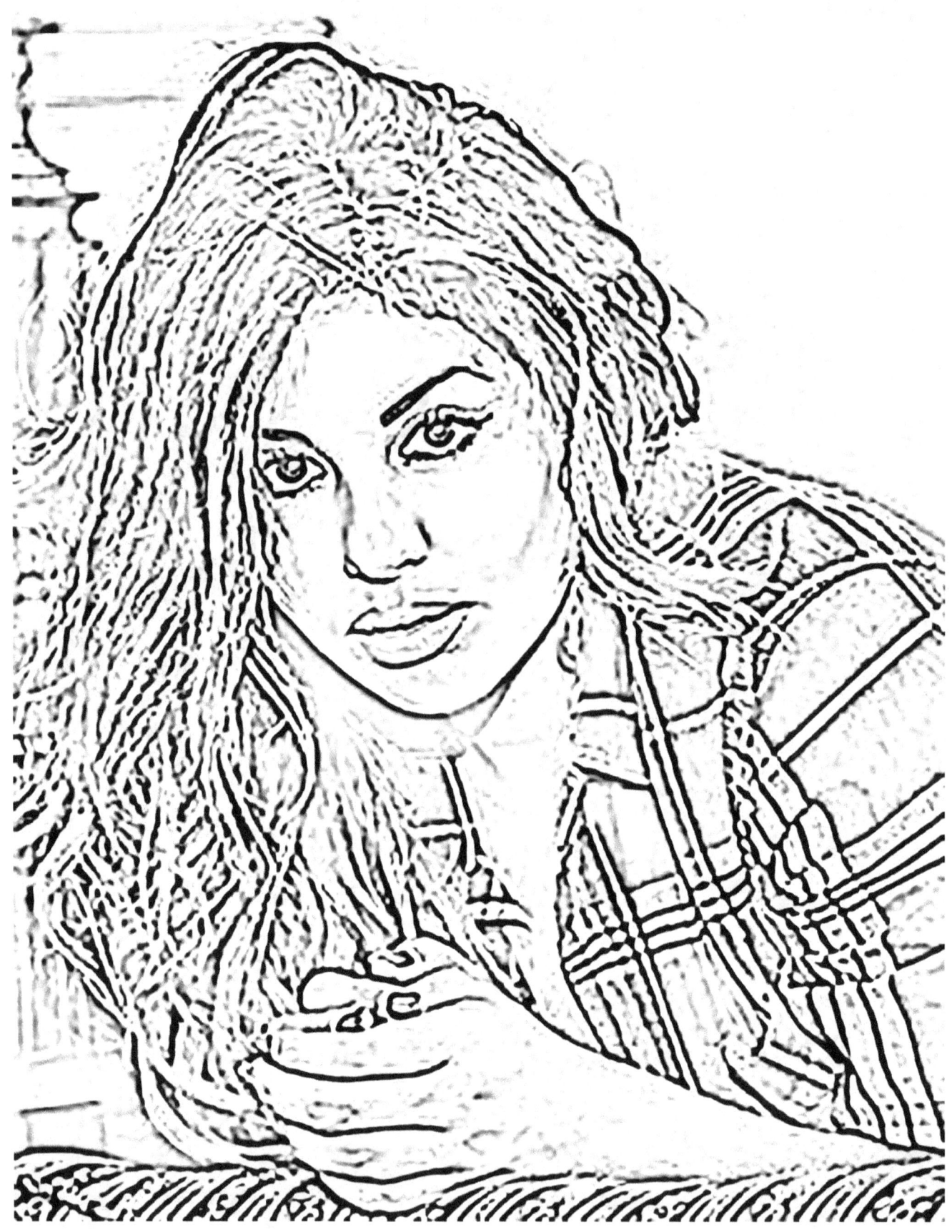

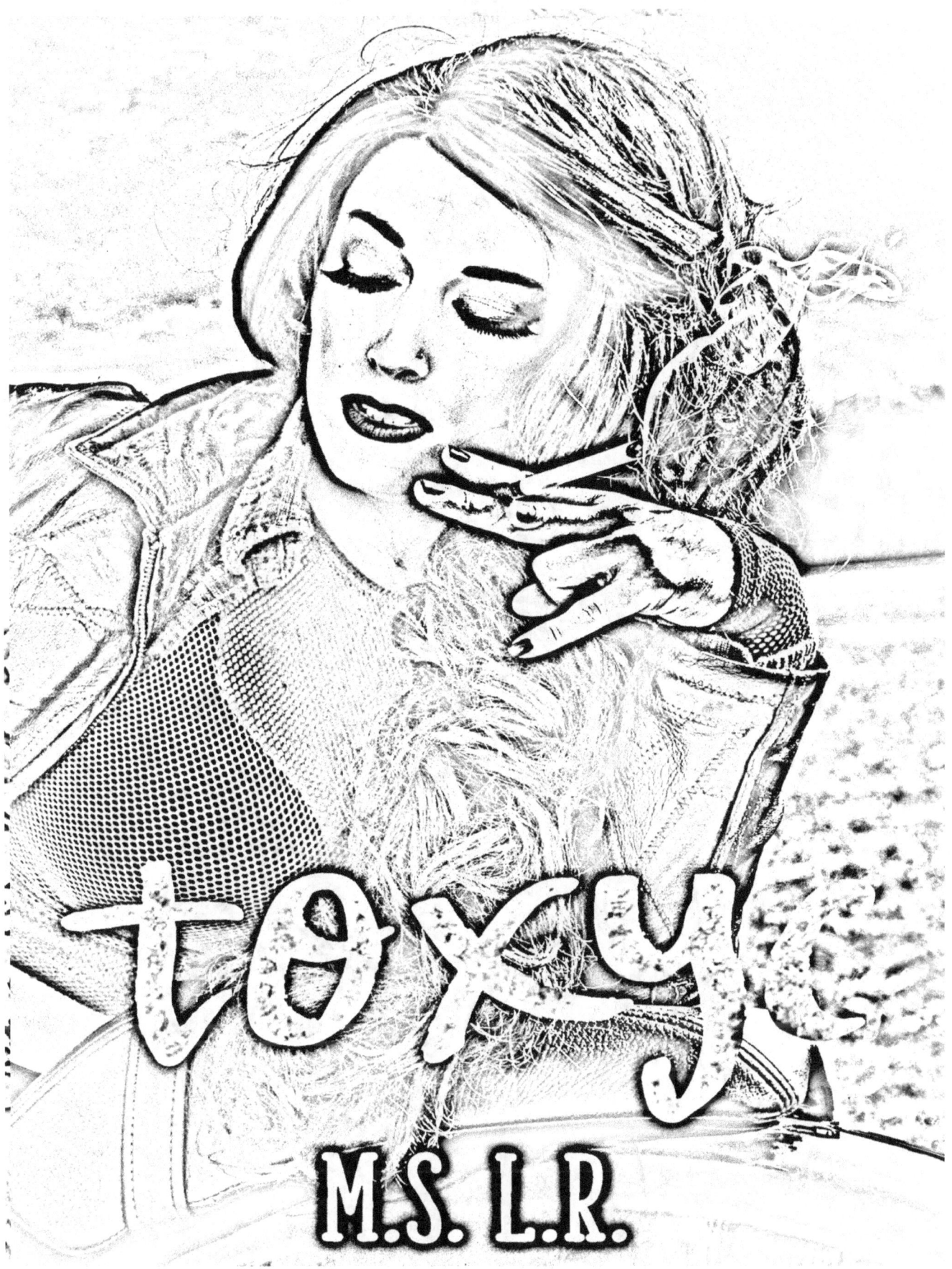

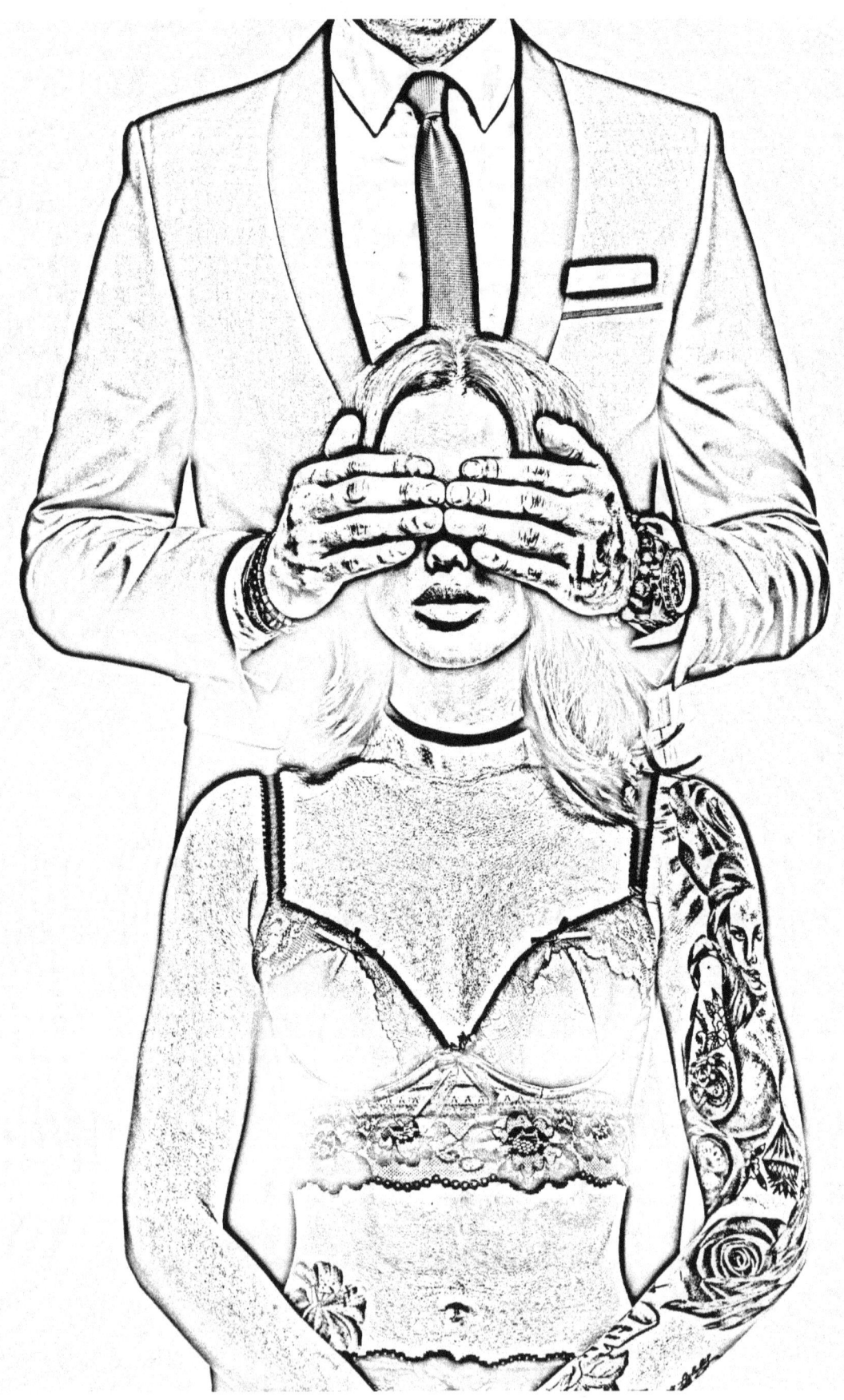

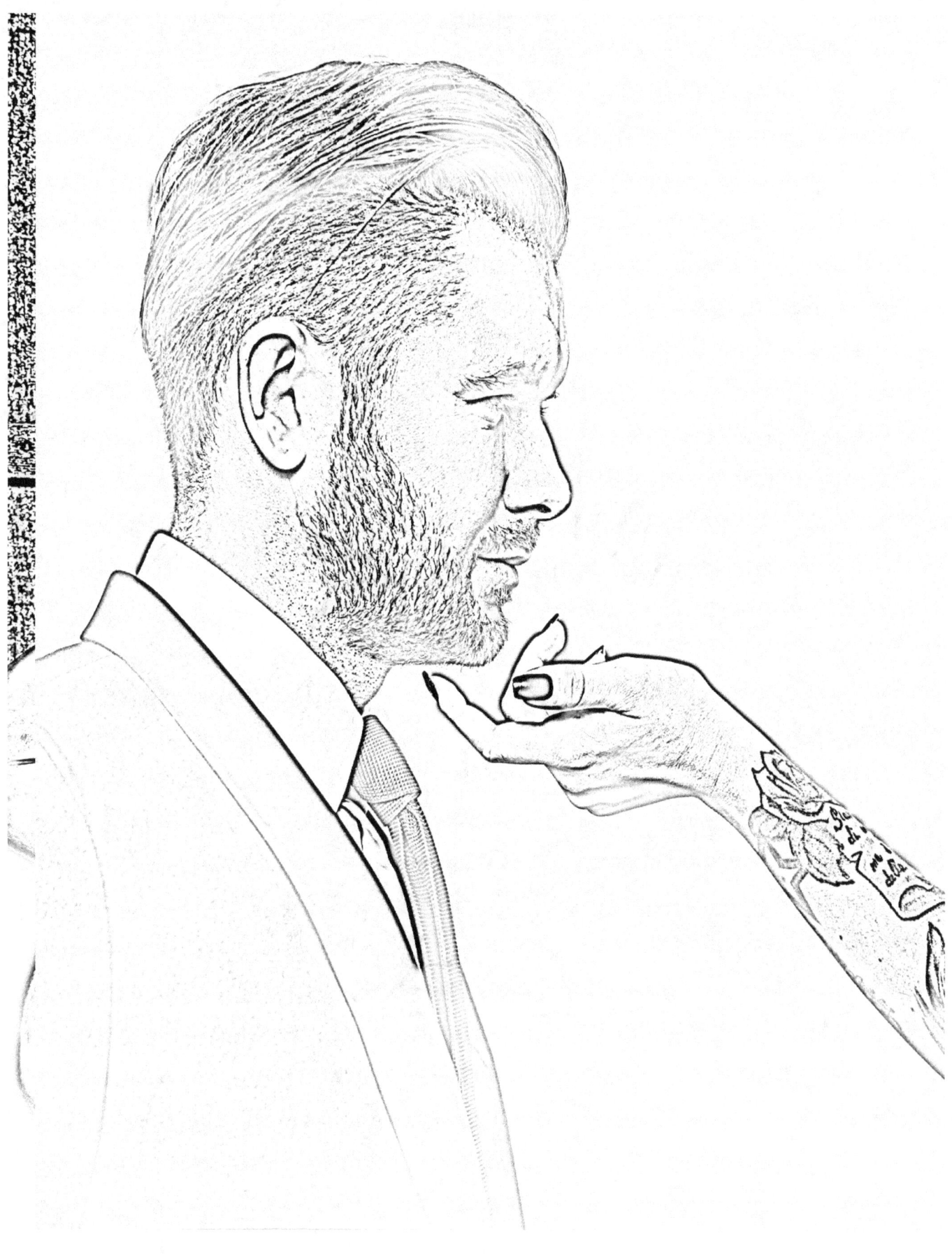

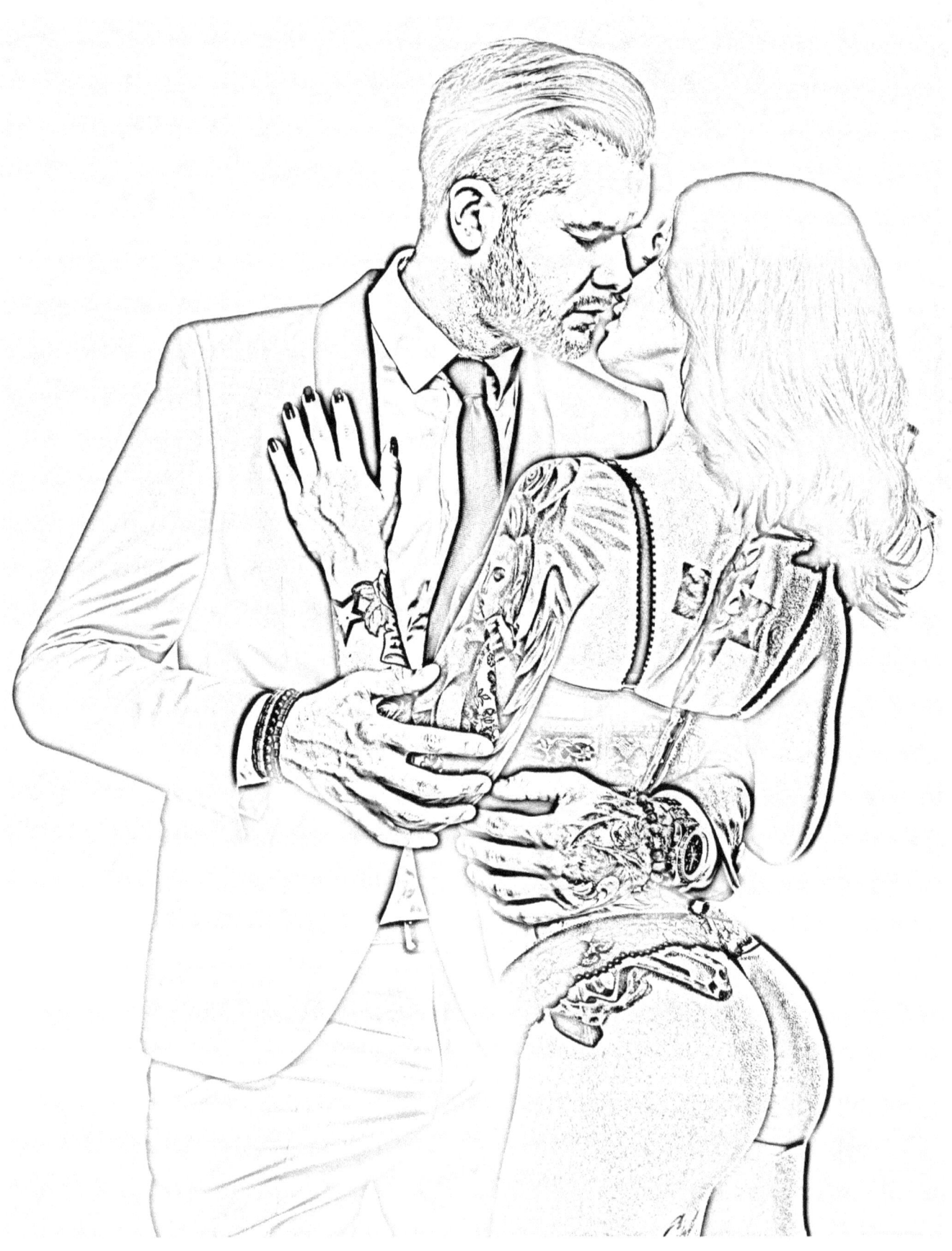

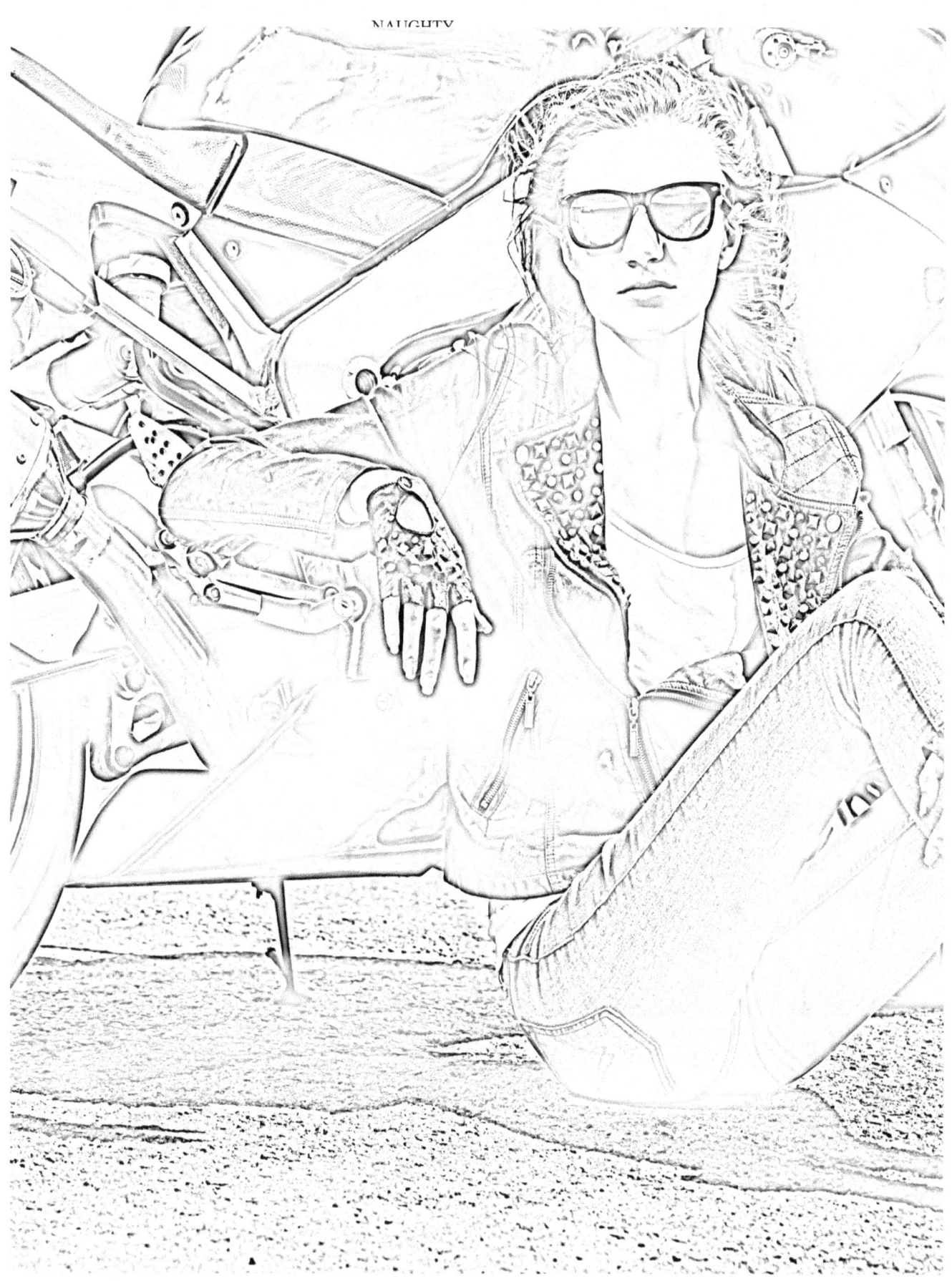

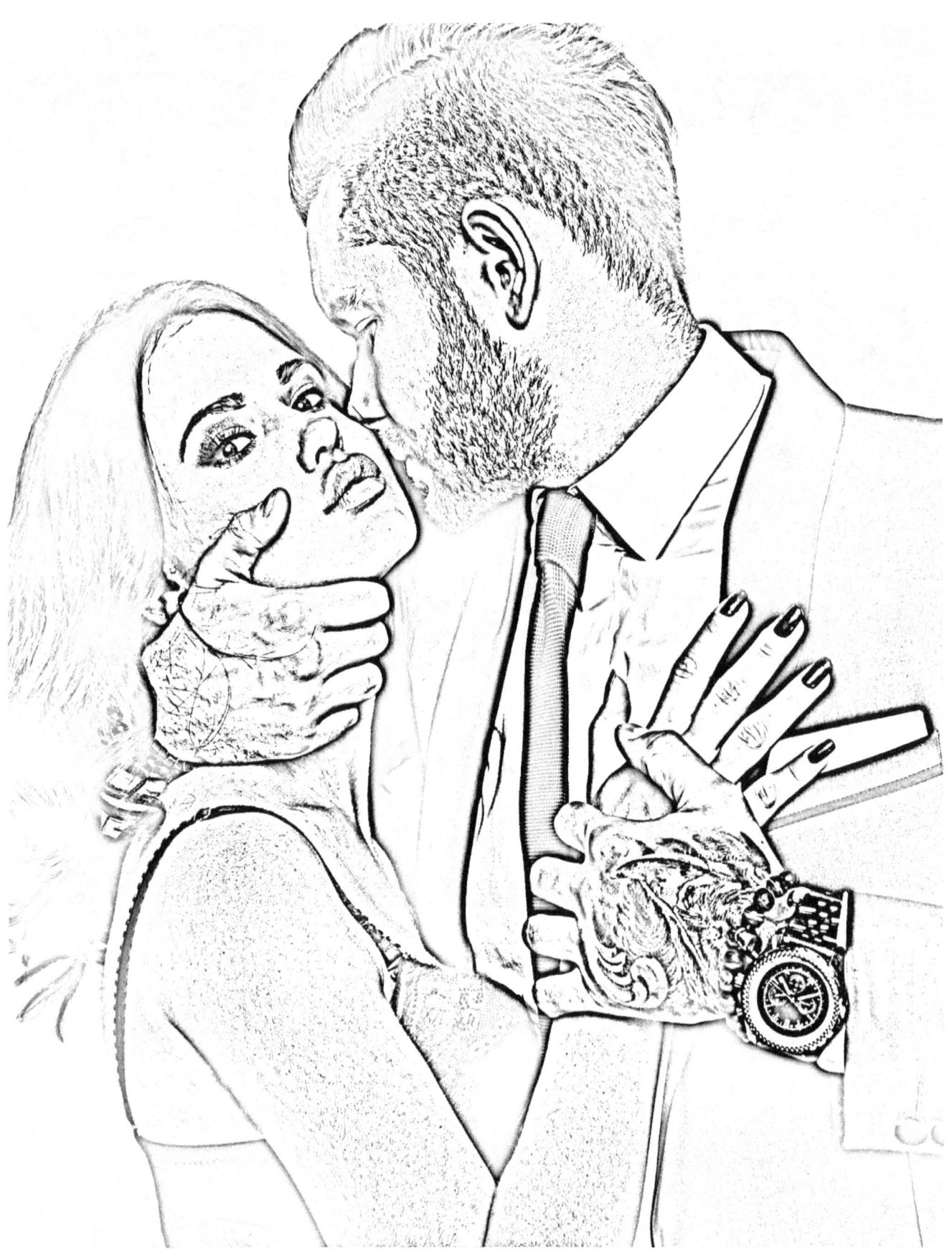

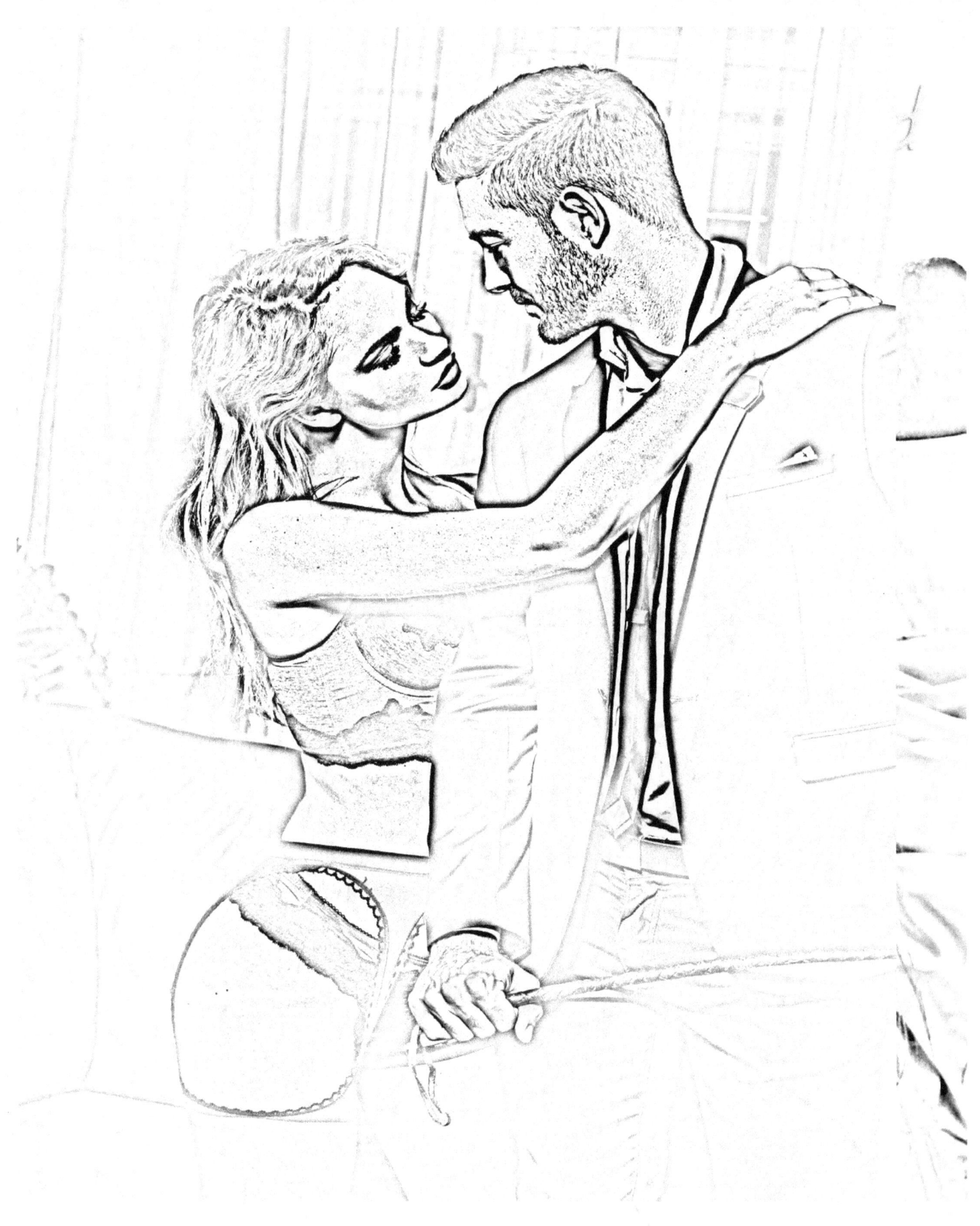

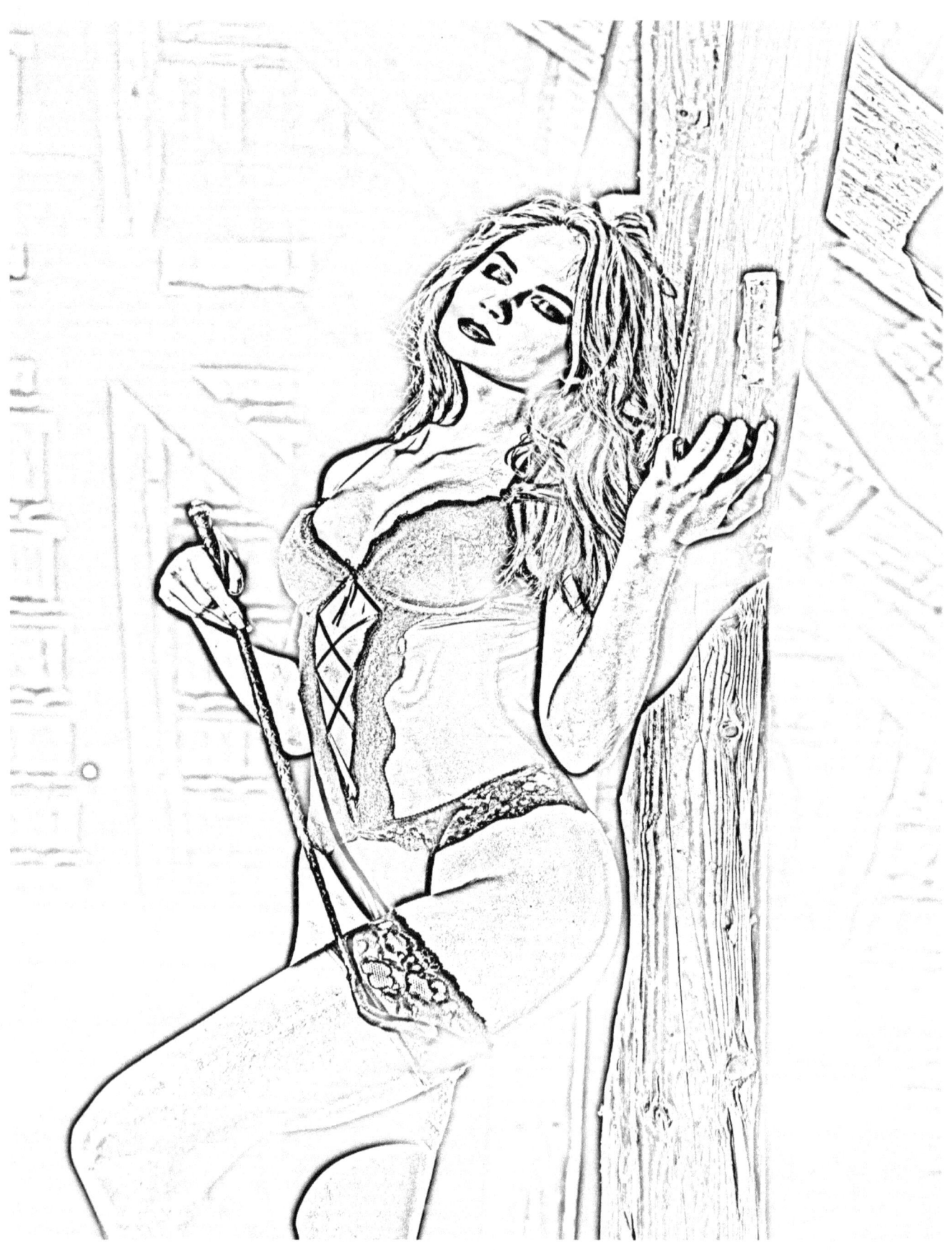

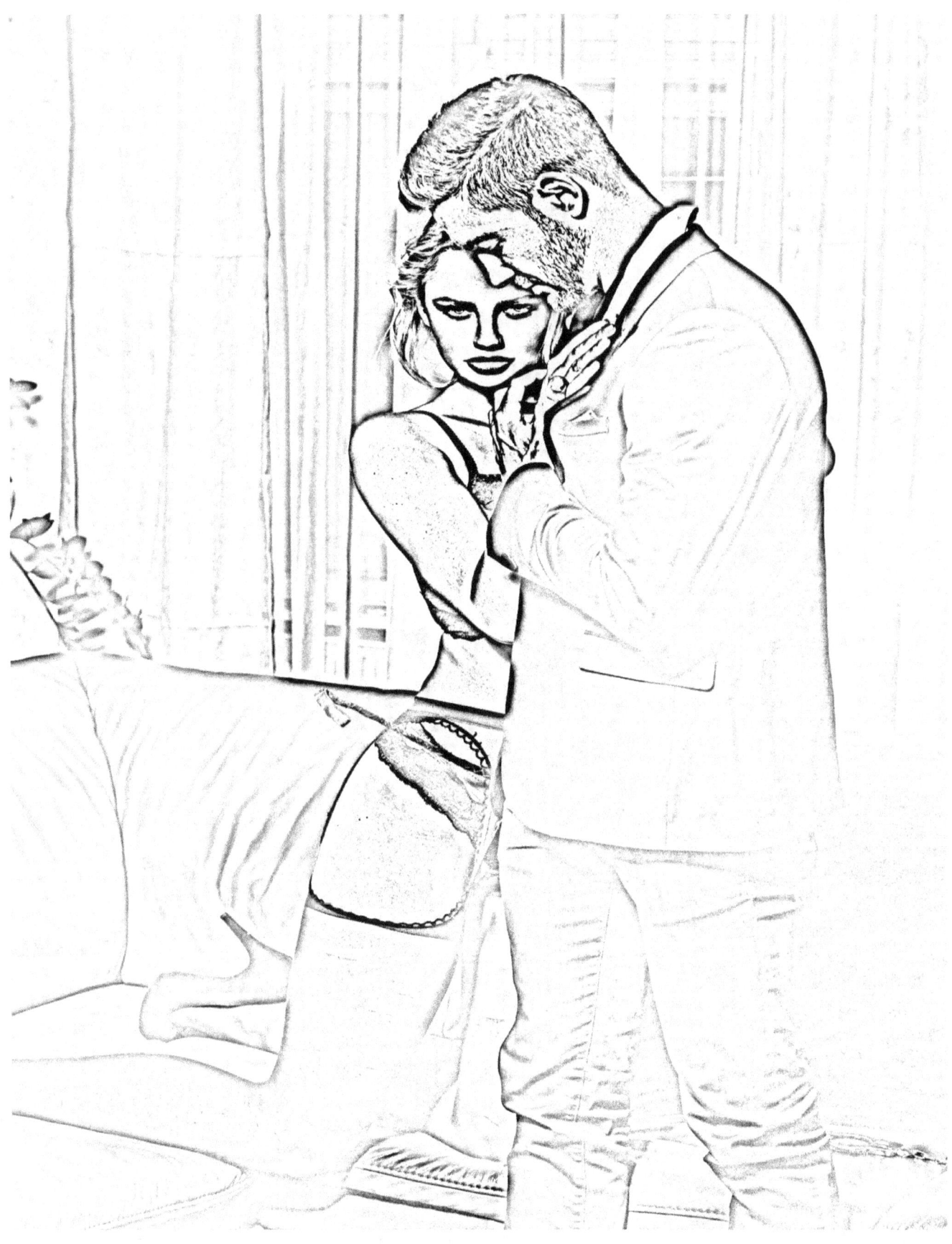

ABOUT THE AUTHOR

M.S. LR. is the author's pen name. She lived in Los Angeles California for eight years and then moved to Arkansas and has been living there ever since. She has a full time office job and writes on her free time.
She loves to read and write dark romance while sipping on wine and eating dark chocolate!

Where you can find her:

Facebook: @authorstefany

Twitter: @StrlngGry

Instagram: @authorstefany

Pinterest: @authorstefany

Snapchat: @s.rattles

Website: www.stefanyrattles.com

ISBN: 1548181811
ISBN-13: 978-1548181819